Claire DeVoogd

VIA

Winter Editions, 2023

SISTE VIATOR

*The fishermen say their enchantments before diving
into the deep to make the fish flee.*

Catalan Atlas

Today shaking wakes me at four, dream
I take you to my hometown, it's all different
Hannibal is there with a legion of miniature
Elephants; oh, that's how, I say to myself.
They're smaller than dogs. Sorry I didn't
Realize it was like this. I don't know how to
Lead you to the water's edge my friends go across
To die in. Sorry. The English is bad. The night
Water there licks at black stones
Like pupils mirrors watch.

Mirrors rattle in their frames, Stacy
Wanting to know about the Taliban—
This is not the war or is it. A glass shatters. Frogs
In the pool. In wartime it's easy for us down
Here to think of love and Britney Spears
Is there, twirling, with her eyes smudged dark with
Mirrors for us that stars reflect. Everyone says:
What is she doing? I'd like to kill her, then
Save her, then kill her, then save her
Then kill her. She is an identical, immediate
Blade. A frog in the pool is dying.
In the noise there is tension as in that
Which compels oil from hot iron, the oath
Taken in strange hands to overstep the burning
Heart. Let everyone save themselves
Like money, air, Jesus, art. What
Are they doing with the general of the enemy?

Pay attention. There are lessons in these
Disposals. Name streets, make fiction.
Caress me, I am a fact. Caress me
To consequence I am a simple fact. The war

Is moving, it is moving around, you can hear it
Upstairs, downstairs, groaning, spitting
Bile in the sink, the sky at dawn is drenched in
Lavish color and this means something—
One or the other, not both. Coral bleeding
Off ornate impediments leaks down. Bones

Sink. Suspect everyone. The frog
Which saved itself laughs deep in its throat
On blue mosaics from Gades. Damask of Istanbul
Is cheap in the chintzy sitting room of an expert
Character sketch. Henry the Navigator says
Characters can't think, they lack power. In India
Miss England with her springtime arts. Speak
Of home, my son. Come west. At yellow
Sunset Phoenician tombs empty
Miraculously of the corpses and are reused.
Scott sits in one to read an American

Novel. This picture, proof. Pictures, bindings:
These constitute the truth. Why must there be
Something underneath this flower
In thought, there is not: the flower is soil, each root
A petal of it. That is what Britney's
Saying. Books obliterated make the gods
Only images the light things take to
Make spikes. Dogs' teeth scrape
Hard on the bone. And in the pool rain
Is boiling water to mirrors, warring
With wet roots that tangle in frogs' legs in eyes
Of gold foil that blink from the sides.

Adorned with huge workforces we're
Building with stone, with granite
Loaves spangled with mica. What is that
Workforce making in the provinces
But suffering, leaping, sparking like particles.
Forms follow one another rolling over
Mountains becoming historical marked
With cairns that mimic them. The light
Begins to spike. This is like a game
But it isn't one. Dido is there. Dido's in Marfa
Reading Henry James. In Port-Au-Prince
Aimé Césaire, feeling with fingers
For what constitutes the face.

A man puts a gun against his brother's cheek
Another takes a picture. At least the President
Knows how to grieve today, reads the paper.
It is a bloodless act, for in his veins run
Syrup, milk, that black of powder, no world's
Coming or enough. Pittsburgh's having a Renaissance
Carnegie a green hill the coal's come out of under
Queen Anne's Lace, nodding pungent above strange fallen
Ground earlier invested, shoveled to Iowa where
Romans fail to profit. The President
Loves trains. So does Neil Young. Airlines
Sell wishes, not flight, says Sahar, the money you have
Will be heaps, you won't sleep. Regulations

Paper borders gone to unclear purpose. Everyone
With their secret information attaching
To their spines. The old men will be mad
Will be made like Britney to dance
The paper dance behind rich screens. Suns

Beyond suns. Can you see the beauty of the place
You are from, Stacy asks, to such a degree.
What does this taste mean but more delicious
Fruit. Peach, peace. Andrew and Abby paint
Drink, have a fight, in the morning their eyes
Soft from crying, sex, some release. Sugar
Settles in Chinese plastic bowls to pastel
Silt, glinting. Strange echo rings. What

About the children? Give them things, suffer them
Into history, a golden charm, teach them
To run, to hold hands. Their mouths take the war
Like earth takes those dark bubbles to
Die in, to pipeline, as veins in the dust bowls
Worm underneath. At dinner we agree
To be eaten, our creature grace simple
In candlelight in winter the Alps
Await a nervous breakdown. To read it
Means to know it, the whole wide whirling mirror
Solar grammars turn to satellite, of silver alloy, alpine
Or another smell, the dampness of brick
Walls. Sentiment fails at spring's end. See

Nothing. Everyone grows irritable again
In the afternoon, wet clothes press flat on terracotta
Tiles, fires start up or fail to start. The sun eats
Blood, don't look at it. Born so large and prone
Upon the tiny ground one hates the sun
How it beats and beats down, its pulse seeming an
Iron mimicry suffusing the universe with color, with
Power, with vision suggesting the right form
Could save you, some archipelago invention, that step

By which to slit the throats of murderers become
A foot to drag behind the beat of all the lurid

Delawares. Beat drums. I wish you were all right
That clouds would stop eradicating my friends
That there were great men who could survive
In history and make the world anew like rain
Does seem to, that the paths the goats walk
Up the Hindu Kush could bring it somewhere
Somewhere not fictional, no power, no one
Had too much, that I had seen it, that I knew
I had, that I always knew what a dream
Was, was a really great man, I could just be
In love and speak every language even the birds'
They'd stop building this machine that kills

Everyone. Here—to things. Here would bathe
Cuauhtémoc, kinged, crossed, alien
Killed in the European style. Cortés, grim
Clerk, doing the soles of his feet big by Siqueiros
For America coming out of the predawn.
Try again, imagine, pray, scream, wish
Shakespeare had written this play, that we
Get ahead of ourselves—ahead of this wave of
Wings, sails, bright tapers lifting and sinking in sea—

Interpret them anew. That holy brand is phosphor
And the gold long pounded thin to reliquary
Cosmological diction. Stacy cutting yellow
Fruit, Andrew laughing, playing the American
Songbook reinvented in cigarette smoke, dens
With flammable sofas where there's red wine

Weak drugs, PSYOPS and assassination in the
Seventies to fictionalize you. You do not let go
Of me. Then that influence mingles with those of
Islamic Iberia. Mercury bitten from soil
The substance of souls, good banana. Now plates
Are falling from open windows. To sing
Of kings make worlds from profane futures ring
On vested stone. Now we are at the beach. It's
Not a frontier. Bloody flag, it is dangerous to swim
Today. Someone is calling is waving from shore.

Simple signs words seem and, seeming, seem to say:
Unspeakable body, unpeaceful doorway, siste, devourer!

ERRANDS

a correspondence with Marie de France

MARIE TELLS A STORY

It is said God has built a simple machine in the center of the ocean. The ideas and colors get processed through it, making time into different molecules factory angels measure finding patterns that tell stories. These stories are things that happen and things that don't. Man invented fiction at the same time as revolution and himself. Reading doesn't make words. The word is a machine for making systems of reading, magical to the degree that such systems may be. Could you but see the aspects appearing all together there where the machine scythes and churns the sunken earth so breathing is invented, you'd become a prophet, and mad, for you cannot tell these things but by that stupefying gap between a metaphor and the array, like blossoms, of their inevitable historicity. These belong to one another. They are in love. Sugar was consecrated to fuel primitive accumulation. Sugar sweetens the pact. It explodes. The walls of federal buildings marble canvases for violent sentiments in purple, brown: immediate, absolute, seen. Necessity grows clearer, a glass flower it's almost ready for.

They want an explosion they describe like an insatiable baby to swallow the earth, to enter reality, which is hell. They hate and fear the old gods because the old gods belonged to people they obliterated who if they came back would destroy them, being huge and disobedient to the order of things as they are today, hating them for having killed them, for being those for whom they deserved to die. It's a blessing those people died that we profit, they say, and live today as masters of it, this hell, which is systematic, and the system of it a way to know hell. To kill a people is to kill a god. To erect statuary. To turn it to gravel.

The old fountain cracked in half with its ancient grammar rubbing away stands in a bus terminal and poor people lie in its shade, among grackles gleaming and leaping in car exhaust. Others have lunch. In this way it grows more and more lifelike.

A people of four may make a community and set about becoming a system to distribute power. The coffee, the dishes, the sofa, the insects and little ecocide in the kitchen; the illness, alcohol, silence, books and paintings and playlist are signs to distribute power. This is a lesson. Anything can be. The corn grown in lines and clusters with its big unnatural seeds renamed the English word for grain is harvested. Another of God's years starts. The corn sleeps in silos in the silent cold time.

When the ocean tries to take you, yell its name, loud. Using the strength of your legs and lungs come back to land. That seed is not for you, not tonight. So I sleep in a church tonight. The waxen yellow in the wings. There are words inside everyone and sometimes they are coming out still green a fruiting bush. Wed in an alley. Where the wedding isn't so loud in the alley we can gather and speak, where the weeds seed and split on air, leap where wind goes. So I sleep in a church tonight, so what if I sleep in a church. So I am weeping, so what. There are houses and the bodies of dead men down here in oak and bronze. Can the trees be ok barely moving in a little watery wind as if their tongues had been taken out. Above the hurricane is skipping across the waves. It will soon break on green land and shatter things. Gemlike the water will jump from the ocean, the great fish will come rolling out with their mouths clapping. It will damage you, take your heart, take your tongue which might be a vine growing out of your heart wrapped around it, a bindweed.

Mulberry purple the ice eddies in, up and down. Black of ink, which is reddish black. And the tomatoes splitting, a tea, red ice and eyes of fish you suck out, and their red eggs in the little spoon in February. We are always waiting in February for something to happen. Then it's March, and everyone breaking up. It's fucking cold on Easter Sunday for ballet practice in the yard. Then everything is broken up. April covers the house in pain, alexandrine, cayenne, ochre, coral. And feathers, the feathers are coming out becoming nests for parrots' eggs. They all know how to read. Everyone does, thinking in the plaint language forms and shades about the millions of things they see each day, everyone does, even the dead do. Their language is sad in its utility, not right away but afterwards. Its afterthought is sad and red and buried beneath the lindens. The parrots' feathers all come up in rows like carrots grasped by the greens between knuckles and heaved, shaken, dipped, sunset, cropped, marked, shaped by a memory of soil, grave rubbings. These fish are coming up in huge nets all fallen together and shuddering, gasping, dying silver. Everything is coming up. The nets seek to go lower, to scrape the soft palate. They think there's nothing to do but scrape. Everything gets poured out and breaks up. The cement is cracking. There's nothing to do but the airport today, tomorrow something else at the airport, something violent.

At night I live in a garret next to a human animal that eats carrion, human carrion. I live over industry. He eats over it. I stay in at night. As long as he isn't hungry and doesn't see me I will be all right. He's pale as apple flesh, long, quiet because he has no language. He can't read. He breathes and doesn't hate me. He knows I am there, he leaves me alone. There are other things to eat. But the flood is coming and the tornado. A great storm is coming and things will change. I'll have to go out. I tell you to be quiet. We'll wait as long as we can.

Yesterday morning the bee starved for the basil, white beads and chalices it touches and pulls away to seem a sorcery the air holds up. How it thinks by hanging itself in the body of air, strange, everything is strange in morning yesterday. Green things with the sheen on them of virgin times. A moss so green it bleeds real blood. A missile range of morning glory in the minefield. Starved leaves come on small as vapor drops and russet mouths between are biting, stinging, growing skins. Inside me there is nothing but gardens. Endless ones, covered in string of pearl, in paintbrush. Material culture lasts a long time in pigment, vellum, rope, ink, glaze. Half-life of silicon 170 years. The matter of our knowledge tells us things, what the future is, what we are thinking it is, what we are thinking, what we are thinking it for.

Early this millennium I grow terrified and weep in the gas tank, to know, in my bowl, the kind of meaning I will be, the million molecules of breath coming to sex, insect, putrescine, cadaverine.

At evening I eat soil from a little spoon. I extend my tongue carefully to taste it and it moves there in a thousand inconsistencies of miniscule and sugar. I take it into me, devourer. The sunset is two thousand variations, all feelings becoming indigo, and the Perseids are falling, drenching, blue stains. One taps on a hill and it lights up orange, a parrot's wing fixed to a shoulder coming down. Kicking there, kicking up and down the shoulder from putrefaction into opening and black while all the words for things are spoken.

The torch belonging to this is a hard thing like a cyst or pearl in the breast, the arm, that origin the liver is, not a line of credit, not something you carry. You only know it sometimes, but it's there. Suddenly it's something you feel, a cut, then a canyon, seeming illusion in the strange and dreadful verticals covered in winglike striation and earthly fluids. No one goes in there, not to that river, not to drink. Then it's not there and it goes away again. Day starts.

I ANSWER HER WITH A MYTH

One day I married, Marie
a semantician. He would say a word
and then say *that's the wrong word*
and go on. Still he was always
talking. I loved him so much I thought
my jaw would break

We were making money-
making syndicates into perfect humans
in the semantic mode, they were full of will
they understood us and were
certain, so deliberate, they dug
so many holes in the ground, they were really
passionate about providing
us with these holes, it was both care and
service—they asked us to climb in

We had cultivated such an affirmative
imagination on our functionaries
having eaten too much yogurt parfait
we were dairy/no dairy people
and communicated like this
till the words seemed to have
no skeleton no impact
they were liquefied
like a protein shake
with the letters and hearts
blent and crimson-bubbled
in that very decisively pearled
paste.

And so we saw there was
no other way and
we climbed in.

BLAZON

Now I have begun I will do my best
to record the rest.

Smelling of lily-of-the-valley
a bus conductor eats his sandwich

on a promenade bench.
Stippled, filigreed, chewing.

One increasingly falls away
from herself. The others

are tethers and the noise
insect. *Sometimes the bodies*

do not fall from the trees
sometimes they do. Some

bodies fall from the trees
sometimes they do. These lay

semantics were like
the air going out from you

dragged out by a super
human hand. We thought

your lungs would collapse
but you know each day

one must dedicate oneself
to the suspension of that

kind of doubt. You didn't die
but lived. Everyone was ok

except for that one
who was dead. The story

was enough to go on
ending for another. Admit

it was sexy when your arrow
rebounded filling

the wound with scent
and deer's blood.

The garden was green.
The world only beginning.

You were so mortal
you were so fragrant

so inflected
by the agony of cure.

You were so indescribable
so worthy of praise

and so on, and so on.
My love.

SMALL TALK

We're going through such heat in the interior
nuts relinquish the branch and clatter
fat parcels squirrels amble through, alien
in the natural city, its living ideologies. See
how tall the trees have become now they are lucid
pouring ideas for the sky from green
glass tumblers the sky merely sits in.

Consider that seeing itself is a faith. Each turn
each mote in it. What do you think about mine
t-shirt, money, question, faith. Know this
is a feeling, not an argument, though sometimes
the feeling is the feeling of argument. In me
there is no new matter, question or project
but everything has always been there, or is gone
including those things that remain unseen.

SQUIRREL TALK

The figure of a squirrel is great
for freedom, the tree, an abacus
speaks a holy tongue, continents
can be refuge, makeshift
sanctuary the globe
thing of pieces, spins
and the city, global
like that, a huge
open mouth you sweat
in, Marie

LIKE NEWS IN WARTIME

You save possible stories
like leather or rude herb
to be boiled in water

We were in the Vale of Cashmere
talking about spring and evil
there were heaps of Damask roses women
were grinding in their teeth to make scents

The Park Conservancy stands on the side of the park
it wants to protect the park from the predations of those it
*   exists to serve*

It circumscribes the park, restores the vale
and may show itself to be noble
in wartime, under fire, people live in it
the park, it's a dog in this way

I believe Marie isn't
she's a motif
which means she can people holes
over in paper or concrete and this makes them real
places or kind of like anchors
around which this lesser
infinity of others and others of worlds and worlds may
    pour

You too see your life like a story
I have heard, and move from
story to story

/

I am the daughter of a sailor.
We're kissing in the park
in secret on top of a low wall
sharing biomes like dogs
leaning back and forth
between the provinces
a glossy car circles the path
watching us. He would like to go home
and give his daughter this vial
of blood, these red beads. I
hail a man holding a metal
rod and he looks at his feet
what's so wrong with being
a dog's breakfast
(asking for somebody else)
there's a hill here
growing greener turf
over the discarded bones
of a few decades of proto-
industrial fishing that were
going on while Marie
was writing this and then ended
without violence, without turning into
something worse. Occasionally
a collar is unearthed. And a blue
cotton shirt. I don't understand
what it means, no one does
a few people have ideas
Marie asks when it will rise
and go back to its god

SOLILOQUY

i.

And at the carrying out of the line
Where the shell man emerges
To suck the meat out
Blow, wind

Each part singly unto itself
One separate blue ribbon
A yellow orb that is felt

We cannot go on like this
You tell me to let my clothes be
Varied of texture and transparency

That my shirt be two silk
Scarves tied together
My boot cellophane—you yell

My name—but I always have one foot ahead of you
Memory splits across that second
Foot, the one that's in the future so

It's hard to speak back to you
Just of the things that happen
You once dreamed a red room

Hidden under the park
You were so sure it was there
And a raccoon who was your pet

You nursed it back to health
It took the things of your hand
In its hand and washed them

Clean. You lived in the trees then
On a platform some men had built
To shoot at deer

Tore your brothers' eyes out
And ate only blueberries

ii.

And the waves lift
And drop me all is
Blue chalk but a bit
Translucent
And the black parts are full of holes
The spray blows from
And the yellow all
Fills it

Like champagne
Water pours from an oak tree
A great wave heaves me
over it

And the umbra at the eclipse
Which with its permanent blade
Cuts the platinum glade
Of mothers, food, children
As forms

Instead of holes
You wish you saw continents
On the moon; we speak then
Of service, the better part
Of him who in the end
Is an individual only
Unto himself or
A computer, full of
Dinner and
Stories.

iii.

In the Exeter Book one
Dreams of the knee of his lord
He is pledged to that knee

iv.

That knee, that knee
Lord let that knee keep him
For it is your knee I love
Dark, peerless
Depths of it
Such that
To think it fact be
Mere credulity.

MARIE CRAWLS THROUGH SOME HOLES IN REALITY

Sometimes a woman
kept in a wall crawls through a cave
in the woods after falling
and comes out of another
that is the same as her own, she is covered
in the blood of a human bird, she can
go back to her birthday
again, whenever
she wants, just by walking down
the road. The present
is the time of the text and
it's an outrage some people
say, though others say
different. Marie does
hers to delight me.
It's a hole in this gripping
reality and the primary function
of it, some say, is the obliteration
of human beings skipping
across the waves between Cape
Breton and the Cape of Good Hope
my friends walk away through it
I lower myself through a green brocade
curtain in the park and wake up
somewhere cold, wet
and without light, I know
it seems unreasonable but
each word contains three
other words including
itself, this is a physical
fact of the poem Marie

is writing, the President doesn't
know about it, very few
people do. If you suffer
from this state of affairs
I will send you to my aunt for a cure
with a letter that she keep you
in her care: in this way sometimes
a resolution opens up where
before there seemed
to be nothing but a hole.

WHAT SHE FINDS ON THE OTHER SIDE OF THE HOLES

On the other side of the holes
there was a red pasture
of flowers made of eyes, hawks
with mortal wounds sweetly
flying, squirrels holding red
flowers in their mouths, whole
cities that fit in the palm
of a hand, architectural viruses
skating and dangling their weird
jewelry in the fluid wind bubbling
across everything washing
the trees and grass, the
lilies risen firmly over it, Jesus
was a crane pecking her chest
open in the nest and
in the margins a silver forest
was growing vine
by vine, no more no less
as Calcidius had said.

THERE

But here it might not
be that way. For this isn't
a real place, like
an estate. It's an
other, an old one.

Now I wish
to go back and
to cross with her
into cracked flag
stones into the park
way, that is the shape
of invention, or call it
what you will, going back
and forth between
the real and the other
or so I have been told.

Marie splitting up
at crossroads at
quarried daybreak
in green fumes

*The world is holes, the
convexed, multiple*

EVER

The flowers growing forever.
The trees rising forever.
The wind pouring forever.
The crane bleeding forever.
The clouds wandering forever.
The fish singing forever.
The flowers looking forever.

CLOUDS

Taking up clods of silver
earth and looking for something in them.
Some sort of key or something.

SURVIVAL STRATEGIES

*There was no question of his returning to his land
and he was grief-stricken, not knowing
what to do*

Marie de France

Origin, not organon, not
A list. Not origin, not

Organ, not the blood on the
Mind, the vessels

Pulsing purple
Leeches and cephalopods

Bodies flinging themselves
In that amber

In the center of
Not continents not

The borders of a blue
Cotton shirt not

Piecing, cutting
Standards and eagles for

Lockstep engorgement
Putting signs in

Thread on pink
Silk or canvas

Sail. Not amber, the bodies
With us forever

Falling, basement
Windows spied through

At evening before
Sores on bare

Feet to run, unsurreal
But not reality

Into all white
Oblivion

In evening or evening
In Cape Town. Not surreal

Sunset in winter
At four not that technique of

Orange
Fading. Not pink

Evening or basements
Not winter, painting

Not cascades not
Acacia or battlements

Swaying
Loaded with orange

Baskets of orange
Velvet. Not velvet.

Not Africa incised
Along ocean's edge

In penguin shit, silver
Spiny fish slicing

Foil shallows and electricity.
Roses, not Damask not

Mecca not Jerusalem
Not roses not Rome. Not

Roses of Mecca or seeds
Of the roses of Mecca

Spilled on the road to
Jerusalem growing

Heavenly scents in
The Valley of Death

Of the Romans
Of the Romans

Not death not death not
Now. Not

Here at the edge of
The world. Not living

Making a living at
The edge of the world. Not

Heads falling hot
Melons on hard wood

No questions left
Not heads falling off. Not

The blade not
The firing squad not

The gas chamber not
The black box not

The outpost not
The jug not

The rag not
The papers not

The checkpoint not
The territory not

The terror not
The closed door not

Jeeps not
Drones not

Pink on bricks not
Smell of vomit not

Crepe not
Gloom.

Not princess cake
Or connection

Pities, pieties. Not western
Plains, not ice palaces.

Not certainty or
Patterns of thought

As Eastern woods
To get lost in, night

Falls, not night not
Renaissance blue not

Perseids falling not gardens or
Prospects or landscaped

Remnants, the soil
Of sailors, sunk

Names lost to
The nineteenth century. Not

Landscapes not sailors. Not
Gardens swooning

Like this. Not
Ginger, carnation

Cadmium red, slippery
Scents, not scented

Heads sinking
Not quietly

Quietly. Not bright
Marvels sinking or singing.

Not living in constant
Astoundment. Not

Day not morning
Not day with its investments

Its output not day. Not
The water which comes from

The pipe not
Dams opening

To flood rivers
At evening not

This water in perspiring
Glasses, glowing

In day's glowing gauzes. Not
These roses, these

Yellow ideas, pollen, shuddering
Desire not desire not

Bees. Not
Knocking not

Quiet knocking
On doors at three. Not

The fist, the bathtub not
Friends, not love, not this is

Not. Not politics.
Not three.

Not power not that
Of the dam or

The boot, the sun
The squadron the

Tongue or fist.
Not again and

Again. Not the heap
The trash heap capped

With grass and
Off-gas tubes. Not salt

Flats in Jersey. Not perfect
Latin. Not the way systems

Work. Not
Work. Not this

Not never
Not never never never

Never never. Not
Here.

Not being not
Here when

Someone comes to visit.
Not this book

Not today. Not
Dinner not

Today. Not TV.
Not screaming

Streets
Not screaming again.

Not quiet streets
Not dinner out not

At a cafe with friends. Not
Again. Not French. Not

Seine. Not this torte to
Rise, the crumbs

Rustling in the
Closed throat. Not never

Never. Not one or not
One or two. Not time

Not time for all things. Not
Time to rise.

Not zero not
That hole

In infinity or
Infinity. Not the vessels

Leaking, not the
Leak into time, not the way

The arrow or the ark. Not
Coffee

Lines. Not quiet
Calls on corners

At ten.
Not sunglasses, not

Travel. Not
Losing things on

Trains. Not
Limitless motion

Rocking back and forth
Going on and on

On and on forever
Unto indigo

Sleep. Not rocking
Not trains. Not

That little death
That hangs

In air to look in
In a face. Not

Infinite species
In spirit or flight

Wasps not flies not
Cicadas falling off

Hot branches still
Singing. Not singing. Not

Wasps. Not the car
Alarms, the new

Oil, asphalt or
Probable outcomes or

Outcomes or
Outcomes, not

Outcomes. Not
Parts not perfection

Not dancing or
Trees. Not that beautiful

Beautiful sound
Of wind in the trees forever

Not heard over traffic.
Not thinking. Not dairy farms

Under slow burning
Mountains of manure

And tires. Not breeds of dogs
Not Levis jeans. Not remains

Not the light's
Remains not elephants'

Bones. Not grief not
What grief means

What it might, not meaning, not
Making that forever

Of grief. Not meaning.
Not stories

Of mountains. Not
Mountains not mountains

Of mountains heaped
On horizons like clouds not

Heaps not heaps and heaps of
Horizons. Not mountains

Moving not clouds. Not fires
In clouds not fires

In Oregon. Not those
In the sea. Not the ageless gasses

Released like
Last groans of the dead

From the still
Of the glass of the sea.

Not the early dead groaning out
Seas in the grass. Not

The sea that falls in
Grass from the edge of

Our world forever
Forever.

Not forever.
Not seas. Not

Grass not tears
In grass not trickling

And ants, ants kissing
Not kissing. Not

Boredom, slow summer days
In Fire Island

Not talking of flowers in decades
And decades of Augusts

At seaside in salt hay or
Dune grass.

Breathing
Not breathing. Not

Of Augusts not
Augusts. Not Sundays

Presence not
Labor.

On beaches not sand
In the fruit. Not oranges

Not value
Or progress or mean. Not

Orangery not deciding on
Oranges again. Not many-jointed

Ecstatic
Cities. Not

Bodies, their types not
The weight of slow muscle

O, o. Not ah.
Not sparkle.

Miraculous inching
To press that heft slow

Not azaleas
Holding red

Above lowing ground.
Not urgent tattoos

Secrets from Asia
Insects learn

Cymbals or bells. Not friends
Not friends lost to

Moving in emerald
Shade not

Fragments, need
Not friends becoming sick

To tell. Not rubble
In the imaginary

Or becoming
Better

Gardens or follies
Reaching for

Becoming different
Becoming lost. Not

The sky to fall down
Here where light

Falls, not to prefer
The light on the ground

Where it is calm
Becoming small

And glistening.
Not that light. Not

Space, not
Space spinning and

Breathing to make time
Not the machine

In Switzerland
Looking for time's

First fleck, not denouement
In particles and

Particles of particles. Not
Stopping time.

Not cutting it.
Not cutting

Money, printing
Not white feathers

Not white
Chocolate in Belgium and

Switzerland not
The stone flowers

And babies
On Belgian buildings

Blithely or laughingly
Not opera. Not

Political babies and
Swords

Baskets or screaming in blankets
Or rushes. Not promising

Nothing of future. Not
Lost hands drawing

Walls on the wall. Not fleck. Not
Nothing. Not problems for

Solving not cones narrowing
Up polysemous firmament

In palest blue. Not
Blue with rubies set in

The margins strictly controlled.
Not purple

Where the sea goes. Not
Purple snails or papyrus

Brown, not verdigris
Not vermillion not

Peanuts not bananas
Soon. Not woad not

For a long time. Not
Rough lengths of

Cloth, bolts not for barter
Or trade.

Not fragment
Of argument

Augmented with sighing
With lovers' swollen sighs

Overheard. Not going
To the laundromat. Not

To the store. Not to be right back
If you wake up soon.

Not dentist or
Sour winds. Not

Cholera measles malaria
Yellow fever smallpox

Ebola or AIDS. Not
Microbes not viruses

Not sickness not
Going away. Not

Sighs. Not wasting
Disease, not love or art

Infection or the infectious
Thought. Not

Tropics, not storms
Not turns or swarms.

Not asking. Not asking
If the language thinks

Of itself or what it thinks
Stuck in itself.

Not asking questions
By which we go on

Speaking and speaking
In unsettled forms.

Not content or
Enclosure or

Either or
Not ether to die with for

Experiments.
Not experiments. Not

One's beloved going
Away not

One's lord. Not
Anymore. Not in Berlin

In the thirties not by foot
In the teens.

Not being done
In Exarcheia later.

Not monastic
Refuge, internment.

Not in the capital
At negative ten degrees.

Not wanting
Not laughing

Not sex
Not you

Not I
Not me.

Not the fleet nature of
Bullets

Products perfected for
Single use solid

Falling heavy and green
In sand dunes, not

One million words not enough.
Not weapons

Contracts making the world
Grind on under war

Going around
To catch on

Decades after not
Decades after

Not natures of things
Not natures not nature. Not

Hitting fast and true
Not taking leave from

The life one loves
Later to die slow

And dry on a flood of
Drugs at the edge of

A desert or wood.
Not to be buried in woods or in

Desert not not
To be.

Not the cave
Resounding

With steel and clash. Not
Trials, mad dash.

Not outside
Not seeing

Outside of things and
Not things in things not

Ideas of
Things

Not nothing
Not in them at all.

Not Titian
Not waterfall. Not

Two million words
Not enough. Not

Justice not judgment
Not fixing the law ageless in

Sacred codes not curing it
Of contradiction.

Not words. Not words for.
Not women. Not men.

Not car culture not cars
As homes in Chicago or

The bay not luminous
Homes come to grief

At quiet Christmas
Behind crèches and hay not

Their dispersal not forest
Growing over not homes

Decayed or homes
Roofed with rags

By the side of the road.
Not food

Culture not vulnerability
Of food not economy.

Not wonder not nightmare
Not spectacle not

Trembling not fear.
Abstraction not

In abstraction. Not news
Announcing

The march
Of the dead.

Not sameness
Of novels, stories

In bed in the afternoon
Not afternoon confidences

Confessions not popsicle.
Not kids not

In the streets not in
School not in the sheets

Not at the clinic
Not alone not

Killed. Not specifics
Not specific ones

Not now. Not
Rhetoric not

Subjects not
Kings. Not devouring

Not Himalayas. Not that unusual
Pleasure of finding

Oneself at
Great heights or

Watching one
Cast low

Not that
Of the avalanche. Not snow.

Not wisdom.
Not wintering.

Not wintering
In Florida, Avalon

Lake Como and not
In Cadiz, not

Congress, Cuba, questions
Coco puffs. Not conscience.

Not ethics
Not counting

Not confinement.
Not oaks, their

Green lace limp and
Tongueless in

No breeze. Not
The virgin

Forest, not again.
Not closure

Or zodiac, surfaces, mysteries
Of flesh or of spirit.

Not these.

EMERGENCIES

So I thought of lays that I had heard and did not doubt

Marie de France

APOCOLYPSE
(as locus amoenus)

Where city becomes a home for sunflowers
wires and wild cats beloved of truck drivers of
the long haul. It's still not over. But the
bloody fountains watering gardens of wood
chips in the dim fall for no one
behind a low wall wherein our waste is treated.
We climb to the tops of some trucks and look
carefully. Still we could not see it was over.

DREAM
(as a riddle)

There are two doors
and two brothers
one asleep and one awake
she said. I looked
where she pointed
and saw the gate
all picked and fixed
with gems. It seemed
more like floating
I was loath to say
it was mechanical
some early balloon
or zeppelin of oak
and pearl, some days.
Many of our common words
are proper names
and they unlock things
shake them up, when used
correctly. It's startling
to hear your proper name
when you aren't expecting it.
This is Rome
she said. It was white
and slippery after
the pointless night. I thought
it was a new moon
on which the gasses
hadn't settled yet
and things and their names
were being demolished

in a vacuum, a way
of starting out.

APOCALYPSE
(as if reality were the premise of a syllogism)

Reality would never be
over. The father
would keep taking
provinces out of his
mouth. The stage
would be what the actors die
on, being of
woman born. The birds
would peck the unreal
grapes they hang
among and scream
with human voices. It may
be semantic
waged, economic
or with hooks
and fingers, blasting things.
Earth would hang yellow around
the firmament
obliterated in desert
places. Someone says *life*
is not green anyway
she is from a green
world and even she
knows this. Color
but some slight unreasoned
stay our pleasure craft
unpiloted would knock
against. The green
shifts. She moves

I believe, perceptibly
between two shores.

She says *the*
directive is both true
and untrue. This is possible
because nothing
is yours. Stop
having things.
Others say
the present in the province
is medieval in the year
of the woman in
the world (or) *be the hair*
in my teeth
(or) *do what*
words do. Leave me
leave me

DREAM
(as Jonah reincarnated in 2022)

I am a princess
the postmodern kind
with many responsibilities
having to do with
my own obsolescence, I
wear pastel wool, hats
smile have Twitter ride in cars
one day for pleasure
I go out in a boat, a storm comes
the boat leaps, breaks and
goes on without me
I watch it become small, tossed
on waves, turn a glinting ball
then disappear. Abandoned
I dive below the surface and
find relief in a cave, a bubble of air
sheltered in ocean too low to
burst. Unfortunately
the cave crawls with thousands of tiny
red devils, cartoonish, perhaps familiar
from bumper stickers, valentines, t-shirt
applique, with forked tails, sharp
little teeth, red horns, they
chatter, chase me, they want to
bite me to death, their claws are like
those of a songbird: itchy, they grin and
holler, making little scratches, no
words come only scratches, I run
jump in a pool of water
I'm treading water and these devils

crowd in, hanging from the great
deep above where the rocks curve
but they cannot swim
then unscrolling beneath me perhaps
with my mind's eye, perhaps
by means of my extremities or tongue
certainly cinematically
I see the huge sea below the sea
of which this cathedral
and pool were only anteroom
it is the forever sea
the one with no limit, plot
or circumference, system, fact
or geometry. Through it
a great fish approaches, his back a map
of sunken continents, stars
studded with conches
and the lashes of those ancient
decadent creatures who linger past
the planets and whose limbs
are smoke. Up to this vent
or mouth I float in
he swims as if climbing
a watery rope and, surfacing
swallows me. I fall down
into the warm, dry cave of him
a cathedral of every pink.
Within are all small living things of earth
bees, ants, creatures that love air and those
that toil blindly in the damp ground. Moths
flutter for the several milky carbuncles
that, glowing, light the place
as moths do for the moon

on earth. These creatures would be
my bread. And I feel in my own stomach
pitching motion and dread, for we glide
swiftly, ride the moving ligaments the sea
runs on, smooth and oiled, as, through constant
turmoil, the fish slides deeper. And I eat
and weep and suffer, to be taken
from life and the world. And it is
with huge grief I discover
there is no where or when to what
sticks around after
memory goes: only its daisy residue
growing endlessly, whitely on
and on. So I turn my eyes to the wall
on which are inscribed
as if carved with a knife
the scars of antique languages
Canaanite and Koine
Greek, dead poetry, prophesies and theorems
in alphabets I can neither
decipher nor speak.
I touch them with my fingers
and put my cheek
to the heart of this fish.

APOCALYPSE
(as an observation)

There's always room
for moving things
my mother once said
that's all we do
letting ourselves become
ornamental
or is it go?
—to start paradise again
here's the boat
here's the desert
you love flowers here

APOCALYPSE
(as men in uniform)

She throws the ball
very high and I
am a kid playing
with a green ball
as the soldiers
stand by. Everyone
plays a cop and
a child. *Enough.*
Yes? I do not
understand. Drink
the deracinated
tea. Divide each
word by ten
by ten and ten.
Sentences sprout
flowers in the dark.
Box. X. The
future sits with its
mouth open very
stupidly on a green
coin with another
question and the soldiers
go by. They are
laughing. The past
is a mythic green
grotto and the
fish/rhino/
human blood
drips sibilantly from
a laurel hung out

to dry on the wire
like a green question
doily and the sun
eats it. *Life is like that: funny
in the end.* I put this
around my finger
and mercury keeps
playing on the table
in the satellite
clusters and soldiers

Enough. This
keeps me in a small garden
window in the back
ground. Each thing is in
the round and each
round grows soft
blue and very
small with diamonds
bricks selves
and platitudes.
The green needs
are shooting from
each fried corpse. *I
took it off that body.* The
discourse seethes so
the rocks are difficult
to see. Pink froth
and calf bones.

My friend is brushing
my leg. He takes my wet face
in both hands he pulls

my hair to see if it's
real. He puts
his wet face on my face
and screams. I am
him. *Enough!* I stand in
the medical position.
To talk. And sway. The talk
like a Black Wave
rose opened black where
the sea table had been.
And the soldiers
walk. Shooting Stars breeding
space suits in silver
foil and delicate acid
etching stroked to
plunder the Silver
Seed then Floating
Comet minnows peck
out polyester eyes in
the wash in the end.
It is comfortable
expensive and unfair.
It is shredding.
Enough.
I am full.
Go on.

DREAM
(as a natural disaster)

Then you find a wallet
with cash in it
some Korean some USD
sticker moons and a photograph and ID
remember you are starving
so keep the cash
later things start to shake
very slightly at first
the blades of the leaves
and things like
a bad connection
    then more.
Some parts get very hot
and burn, some cold
or fill with water, some fall
we live at the end of
one wing of a mall
that is also a suburb
and the world
where people shop all day
    for fun.
Next door the Obamas or Bill
Gates has his swimming pool
    you don't
your parents, who are a child
    in this, a
1950s dad and TV
blonde, say
    they are getting a divorce
because of the swimming pool

you are an Honors Student
and win a prize
and Reality that
store
    goes on, ending

APOCALYPSE
(as we drive north)

Qualities being
chicory fade
white beads
dinner, tagine, a
hollow plate.

The lace of the green sea
after the ceramic
shells. The certain smugness
of the shell man saying
ceramic is hard enough
for centuries. The
divers. A bee
in a ceramic vase.

Inner points
scuffs. An IED
three sheep. Art of cracking it
and eating the flesh.
Staring solemnly
at the white camera.
Some people.
Displacement of vessels
with the air bottled
inside them. Gracelessness
at dinner. Caselessness
in the middle centuries.
Facelessness at night.

You spend your days
with an allegory of granite
chipped from a silk skirt
pressed by such and such a
glacier, it organizes
your time, you are blue
you are blue with it, and
roadside with candle shops
gas stations, stationary, antique malls.

Pizza shops, Rams, reliquaries.
Aspect of some real place
in pencil or the white tissue paper
used to blot the grease.

Some qualifications.

Nothing is not made
incompletely
of what isn't it

A day is nothing like
a basket of rolls

A city is never the same, but a vertical
fracture super-minutely refracting among
a moment that continues to recede and
remains, indifferent and never
the same.

A friend's child
dies. The story
declares itself

gamely, a sequence of terms
awaiting interpretation
a series of tents
red, blue, yellow and greenish grey
like a face sick on the waving of sea flags
you saw in it, having swung perversely
by your throat to the left—
a sequence of tents in the desert silk
flags waving gamely.

APOCALYPSE
(as a housecat)

And left—there's a tube of something like butter in
blue that rests on the lower hill between strands, orbs and
the cat is doing something else.

Things cut off and float on rims of others
some you know by the shape of them (binoculars)
and some shapes are how others (centuries)

become separate, solid, take form
from surroundings (cures, wars, the powerful
sweeping down out of mountains

or from the north, on horseback
or infernally, set into scaffolds
of doing the same thing over again

with no difference, whirling or dragging, hanging).
Now the cat is doing something else—sitting
darkly in angles, breathless, the hair

on its back slightly raised: starlings, take note
pause in thy awful plunging
pouring earthwards, deathless, through the gold

units, through the white units with which all
is decided, all finished for now. And the
sharp quality of the heat units that stand still

behind. I once read that almost every farmhouse
in the Northeast at one time kept a copy
of *Inferno* with the engravings by Doré.

This is surely an exaggeration, but did find one
once in a wooden chest at a cleanout near Syracuse
in a red clapboard house that was coming down

along with the farmer's diary bound in red leather.
It was terse, the book, most of the entries having to do
    with
weather, but for a week or more in late winter, 1887

each day read: Shot a fox. *Shot a fox. Shot a fox.*
And the point holds, *this* kind of world
having a round, a certain significance for *that*

with its doing of things in the fitting they have
how the hook fixes the frame, the tongue
the premise and how it seems, then, to summon

itself wholly, more than, even: a fine system
totally, with the fox shape coming out of a dark
area in the white wash and being

shot, day after day, the earth turning
over in damp agonies, the cut worm
again signifying spring. Now the shape

is almost too dark. It blurs. A lecture
can be heard—archaeologies of something
or other, cremations, teeth of dogs.

APOCALYPSE
(as the great year in review)

All the stuff, splitting, the dark seams
before it feels both good and bad to be
so much in the know
then it's two thousand years

gone and there's nothing to it
you see the stuff corrodes
so they can't read it
us, traces of a huge city

or this global inclination
this hysteria in the parks
with the lilacs weeping
salt, silicon reason

Morning is still coming, larks
every day till the end
of the world, the other one
where the sun finally replies

before all the stars in the sky go black
like guttering candles
some New England patio some buggy evening
reporting back, time, after it

ends, like shot
the volley in the grey
stems—a black-eyed
creature in later woods—

that is, the Copernicans report by
aggregate projection this
gutting, this glittering fact
one might keep in the

throat, piecemeal among
the final bacterium of all but
eternal life digestively
its burden: repeating

APOCALYPSE
(as a mystery novel for young readers)

Some absolute again
approaches the meridian
unique, the gold bar of dry
grass at the center of what was
swiftly becoming a swamp.

Somewhere in a glass
boys running around town
looking for a missing treasure
under each streetlight, each avenue
and needle of silver tinsel
armed only with their wits
to take on some crew or cabal

malicious, obtuse, greedy, bright
boys of the sixth age
the unreal one
the one that would come after this one
ends, which is what is meant
by this phrase, this resigned
turn of the hand.

The world it describes
is contraband.
A near miss?
A project in missing
the point of things. We might
burn the records and crush
the gems to powder, throw them

into the Seine—*then what*—
Then what happens then happens
then, again?
                          These strata
were suspended in a chaotic abyss
till Chaos became
the name of that road
the sheep followed
out of Tartarus, jangling.

APOCALYPSE
(as abyss, a complicated pattern)

Allow that this
matter may weave
over and over itself
as a tide, gray-blue, perspicacious
as tides are on the shore
beating, in recession
and advance alike.
This tide of silver
chiming, as the wings
of birds in reliquary
forest, where birds
live when they have died
in Latin marching, Latin
diction. Or in wood.

The whole wood
that turns, the earth
that overcomes itself
season by season
spring into spring
coming over the hill
hospitably, pouring
as water does, a host, full
of bubbles, becoming
condos, white, where
meadow was, quiet
now, uncertainty
coming off it, lightly

APOCALYPSE
(as nature copies itself)

The festival lights
on Ebbets field, plaster
hand, Izmir kebab
thing of unnatural
scope, luminosity
its velvet very deep
gray but not spiritual
just a kind of sentence
seeming to evoke
the delicate feeling
of a mathematical
proposition, there is
no moderation in these
terrible endeavors
marrow shuddering
in the pot, the knife

like cut in the film
each year in the
Roman calendar should
be documented visually
like this movie does
me, it's so hard to be
in time any longer, August
with the hydrants streaming
the water slapping down
the singing underground
and flickering out
of the parking lot

APOCALYPSE
(as ekphrasis of resistance across nature and centuries)

Nature loves hexagons
says Luned in the stone
garden. I sprout
clean-shaven
like a crystal
tooth to grain.
Noguchi gets
his invention from
the stonecutters
by the cemetery like
what's-his-name. *More.*

The word is / so poor.
Heaven is running
in the thistles
downhill. Kite-
like, how the wind
cracks the bold
cheek. Cousins cut
his flag open it steamed and
the pipes were burning
long whistles rose
in the brake
and field to field
like this and like this

APOCALYPSE
(as copies of nature from 1381)

Data freeze in cut frames
rolls burnt in the narthex
Cousins by the bridge
goes missing in the spring
chewed open. Show us
your insides and let us name
the color of your evil
deeds. Below the death
silks fluttering. We're
full of breath and
ravenous and a little
comes. You're ingenious
and quiet beside a stream
of readymades. The spring
parts green

from green. It wasn't
the first time. And a little
comes. He who sat and asked
her that she sit
down naked and
cross-legged with him
and lock eyes, he who asked
that they discourse naked
by the eye, he who was
losing it again. The spring
is a mad time. The gardens
neoclassical austerely
wait. Outside Austerlitz
by Avon. This operation

is wasted, we're so over
it. We want a pure
moral form like a triangle.
One that doesn't turn over
like that when it comes.

After Katerina Gogou

DREAM
(as if a dream were the same as a day)

I walked an industrial
part of the city
where form and chaos were grown together and become
identical to one another.
It was today.

There was nothing there but the yellow clay

    packed hard

    with yellow stones

    and hot

and the yellow trucks
working endlessly

    endlessly. So I went

to your mother, today was
her birthday. She lived in a house
an oasis of sorts
between two factories
near the condos going up.

Every birthday your mother makes
a sculpture as big as
a room out of
papier-mâché.

After Bernadette Mayer

APOCALYPSE
(as the gods think)

Here, in the desert
on the plain
on the moon
with the desert moon plants
growing out of the holes
in the sun
in the hole in the sea, here
in the cave
in the sea in the concrete
sea. Here in the desert
whitely the eclipse
quietly.

After Ezra Pound

DREAM
(as the boat)

But that is water, and I the unsure, un-
believable sense, to see as
though my eyes were changed
by the taking off of
habit, that habit of waking up
myself at blue day's
start, at whistle, was rapt in
such turquoise consequence
to see, as solidity dropped

from matter, becoming
below me all deliquescent
and teary brine, and I the boat the spine
of which cut down
and delicious shot along to meet
itself again behind—that, and under
that, the sunlit, moving place
we traveled over.

APOCALYPSE
(as the sun replies)

An eye doesn't contain an ideal
anything. Not a boat, that
paroxysmic leaping end over
end by which twice
you died. As if
you could see it empty
of you. Knocking. You groan, spit
up. *Do you think I'm supposed
to be me?* The sound
pushed from your still
lung by a more powerful
hand. One, that philosophical
animal, seems to feel a singular
expression. It need not
be said. The world seems to consent
to end, being perhaps
eclipsed again
in figuration, desertification or
colony, eclipsed then a million
a million million
rivets crunching the
century that computer
again and no more
returning. It need
not be said. The bare fact
of hunger. Again a green
blade unbelievably
rises again. White hot
California. Creatures out
of the cages entering

households stony
near legible array

After Henry Dumas

APOCALYPSE
(as aphorism)

True, being a poet, woman, man
and person may be only daily
impediment, thick, mixed, like
syrup. The world
is sweet, still.

The real world. There is
good in imagining it
how it breaks you in half
in the park, or how it opens up
and swallows you, or again breaks
in half over the bad
toast you bring me in bed
that tastes like jam on cardboard
so again I must accept
that you love me
and it breaks you and swallows you
again. And you go on

APOCALYPSE
(as errata)

How do I say this
let it be nothing if it's not first delight
pleasure or a joke a
kindness to yourself something good
to touch. Where it ends
may take your heart
but until then it sustains it. Courage!
that is what I meant by
we are toast.

I thought this
while you were in my throat.

APOCALYPSE
(as a fine system of disks)

It is crisp on a fall
morning.

It is gone
in a revolving door.

Well yes the century
is a very long date.

We come to
on the shore we know
not where.

Well yes the coral
all has sex in an instant

releasing its spunk
into the general ethos.

A form
rises out of the sea
is cut in two

becomes two forms
in two seas

and each untangles
her hair.

Simple science,
that administration
that visits

In all living
things, bearing two

Jello salads,
pop of
copper color.

Simplex
is cut in two
becomes two colds

on two poles
is stretched

on a great wheel
written into the will

for pluralities
to inherit
by the lever's pull:

crest, history
pull me forward.

On the wall there is a date.
Above the date
there is a mirror.

Where these trucks come in
by stony riverbed eagles
and wild cats are talking

chewing over
issues, pledging something
some final thing

DREAM
(as physical frustration)

I wake from the motel
couch and find I am
angry with you. We walk
over a rocky or barren land-
scape and through a
deep wood to the interior
cemetery rising
straight up some sheer glass
postmodern architecture library full
of pink sunset and radical Majorcan
students studying tessellations.
The signs are in English
we read in Arabic there
are three ways to go up—I
sensing us flummoxed
suggest the design of a new
device which would serve
as a method of capture
to impress of the culture its
ambivalent revelation. You
interested for a moment
studiously betray a
studied disinterest, turn
too carefully away
I feel myself stutter and
flutter, wink, fret
tear up the staircase
in a rage

After Laura (Riding) Jackson

APOCALYPSE
(as in a nor'easter, the plague)

When something goes out
a bit like a gesture into
day, the most mundane kind of dream
one gets coffee, looks at a shell
dog walkers in some green surf
with their dogs walk
distantly while this vent snaps
like the ghost of our condo
when the wind goes
howling, and has a post-it note.
An hour is a steel measure.

Then in the carrying of computers
up and down some stairs
a weird smell:
spring perennials
and it's only the first month of the year.

One should acknowledge
the people with dogs, bikes and coffee
walking fast in light steady rain.
Do it only with the eyes.
Everyone knows what that means—
We are in love?
Yes, for the last time.

I point out a fox. Why keep this prominently
a painting so much the same as the view?

Look out the window.
Heaven, it seems,
is something you must do
over and over again
and that's fine, like a question
that connects to another
that's identical to itself
in shiny, primary colors
called pleasure.

(Or maybe you hang out for a while
in arrangement, catholic
and draining, waiting
to catch your breath as the cosmos
is compiled around you, in the echo
where it hadn't been before
and the new glare, the flint
congealing ionically into
these flakes, forces and
cones of forces?)

On the hillside
cooling we were naming our sun
and all the conditions of blue
chalk nested; unlike animals
lay down with each other that day
boosters for real life
and it was real life
and fine, and finished.
Polished?
Plastic.

Or let what happened before
not be in this one. For
it was wet, and so fell to pieces.

BOUSTROPHEDON

—where was there such a world?

As if something poignantly final were happening, or had just happened, or was about to happen, that one could not fail to understand—

Laura (Riding) Jackson,
"Reality as Port Huntlady"

One

I write this as you lie in bed
Like Maya Deren maybe
In a bar on Franklin

The great curve is cresting upon which
Love you're resting

Drive forward, history, with all your false
Coats and baritone devices
In the heart of which a beating
Thing.

Indulge me this is not form.
I will be your author.

Last night I sat upon your chest
And let the gods do all the rest
And howled *Alcyone!* in your mouth

On the mirror there is a crown—
But my love you're resting.

Let you love the bright devices
The system is so corrupt with.

I am with you. Spine, arch.
Me too I cannot wait the
Drag of history.

Maybe on Tuesdays I can write
Not waiting the diversions or the dread.

In mornings I am your friend.

Or take me instead who wish
For a national voice to disparage you.

Oh I will be as stupid as the times for you.

I will postpone without delay
The deposit of this
Trick I call myself.

There is the cartwheel, the chrysanthemum.
I am crisp on a fall
morning.

Would tell you the truth
As you do me: my love
For you is device
Like that.

Like any English subject
Feel you the power of the charged
Line. Like

It is for me and thee and thine
And go down concretely among
The lines, and rimes, the Rhine

Where landbound
No longer men had walked.

The curved line
Is the fire escape, whose

Syllable seems so benighted

Wasn't it always the spirit
Whose empty end is the empty air.
Whose what?

What then. Then what is no longer
Between you and me.

This peach is called a plum, or
Here, the point of this statement.
On this ovate curve, this marked
Wrist.

This is not whatever school
I dared become. *Fair.*

Ceyx lost his life at sea, that there
He stood both skin and being
In Chaucer. The Englishes assume
They do and ride

The line along till it is dead
And long, and gone. And the love
Object who on a table is singing
Songs, in a blue dress, who is
Loved, and lost,

    And food, and dead

She may take off her head
You swoon and fall right down.

.

The flesh of the century is a white hill
Beside the ribs of the earth. I recall I was drawing
A pattern of several circles which
Rode forth

One after another in scales that decreased
As my finger wrote longer and more distantly
On the table of dire conditions, of wealth and deprivation

In this century

                    Of sprawling
Conditions unscrolling apocalypse
After apocalypse in bounded
Infinities, pavilions, public
Parks and forums
In this or that
Century.

It's hard to remember what you said.
I might have had a dream
And wrote this.

Sometimes I dream my mother
Yelling and crying: a dream is the most vivid experience of
       your life
The ship that shifts, wrecks and goes on
While the person sleeps is that. Is that
It.

Well yes the Devil is in the ocean.
Well yes the will it drives you even still you know not where.
Well yes it takes a million corpses
For a dialectic.

The measure of my pet is a rotten
Thing going down. She roars with pleasure
Licks her paws is very warm.

Is a hooked thing.

If sound is an angle we have every
One. This century is pure pleasure.

.

Two

You sleep below a mirror like Maya Deren and I love to
write your dreams.

There is one where I am two people the sleeping one and
the one who wants to kill you.

There is one I myself have died and you are the one who
sleeps.

One we are in some crazy situation somewhere off-world
and the solution is forthcoming.

One this lazy kind of day on your chest in the park you are
always breathing.

.

I do not want to go under the earth in
This century in which we are cells
Holding molecules atoms and the spaces
Between they call dark matter that is
That which does not exist and will not be
Quantified but that holds the universe
Apart so that we can exist as a concept
For mathematicians and lunatics wanting
To imagine the infinite as a place we can
Go between our hands, I do not want to go
Under the earth in this century where the
Places are divisible by axiom, slogan
And common knowledge tells us the mall
Is dead for people to gather in, though
The ancients still pacing the halls
For miles and miles each day they tell us
In pictures speaking the gerundive ways of this
Century I do not want to go under the earth

.

The world like this created thing
Full of chrysanthemums for my birthday
The rust colors of it are
Where my brother is in the earthquake, in the
Illness with the stone in the living room
I will be there soon and take it

.

With chrysanthemums wanting and three
Shelves in the trash I came to meet you
They were curved slightly and mass

Produced. The thing was like
It was a flower in a corporate
Lobby. I wanted a particular
Dress, an organic complex
But I loved the words.

Come out of your basement
Door and make a pledge, it is the only
Kind of language to be loved, manager.

I believe now that the only way
Possible is INVERSION. Those who cannot read
For the white of the page is all that may be seen
Let them come forward.

I believe now in POSTPONEMENT
constitutive, book upon book

I believe now let none speak the whole thing
Is gone a certain terrible wreckage.

.

So tonight
Will go out for Chinese food
To the corner where

The attitude is one
Of acknowledgement.
You are resting and undead, Marie

I will eat inside
From the rain and what
Write.

The earth
One may go on basically
Into should not be so terrible.

The thing will come down that comes down
In the basic encasement for me
You and all the dead

Stuff and fires. Fires are dead trees and
Animals walking around
And thinking, eating, believing

Willing and dreaming
In the present whirling
And totally out of control

We are never certain
How far away you are and think
We know so many things

We have read. We are fires
And dead, like English
Combustion engines.

Dear Steenie, dog
James, dear
One, how many pet

Names has the king
—But the writing
Of love letters is

Not relevant to the state
Of being a fire
In this century.

     .

Then what. Whatever
For all description, let
Revolution after revolution
Come quickly and more
And more. But let it be
Revelation. It is

Today. There is a condition today
Like the hole in the center of a paper
Bill a needle once speared for keeping
And it stays open on the century and if it's so
Open why don't you go through it
Already.

Before the whole thing goes
To worms, foxing, dry
Rot these things don't last that
Long really.

Say nuclear
Then what. Then
Linger. Stay

Over, stay forever like this in the white
Or red heart of the heart of this
Century and when it fails replace
It, like a Rockefeller. But believe
There are certain things that happen
That you do not have the eyes for even.

.

Stones clock calves, thundercloud-like
Rose brake by the substance. A mound
Of it may shortly be made available. To wide

White oblivion. There are three paths and one rings
The pond. And a hundred fifty
Busted tires, each a dollar. From the lean-to

The landscape comes to form
And it is for you, the one who goes around
The holes where there's no traction

In mines there is a kind of dusty
Velvet brown. There is a love that brambles
Act, they are a perverted bush

With five petals to the bloom
And a golden crown, fraction
The bees delight in. And later snakes.

There are wet moving eyes on the deer
And black eyes like bombs and webs.
Starred eyes. There is the pulse of the web

In a way that is fun for the spider
Who is a kind of sailor of the bough.
And species of glass, of air,

And caught, in net, in dolomite, in cabinet.
There are digging things
Seeing color through skin.

.

And came to meet you.

      Tree, mulberry, the fruit

Bursting, staining, that crane

Touching off

      On someone's lit window. Or

These ones with the white froth

          That relates to the mouth

In the action of breathing in spring

And sex, the tree that thinks

To smell of sex in spring.

The qualities
Effluvia and dread
What said one
Another said, at joint
Sap, sandpiper
Snapping

.

Wreck
you make of the bed,

Glasses you leave on top of
Books, Marie

There are a million
Worldly crimes

You could die for
Today,

Each one worth
What in the end. What

Is. There is more money
In the world than there is money

In the world. Little remains
Between you and me

But paper, and mark

And city

My love you are
Resting

I am writing this

.

Three

We turn when the earth turns and blue
Marble comes up, strange thing
Tatter of cotton shirt
Dark with earth

It may come up
In riverbeds where groups
Families, maybe
Turn earth
Over for silver
Food,

In another century
Or talking, I may bring it

Nothing is immaterial, nothing,
My love, the matter; we must
Only open it, turn it over. Timothy
Dear, Solomon, King
Sweeney,

Can any understand this noise

Interrupting the invention of earth, starlings
A chalk line recoiling and no
Edge to the letter

Which would be where the world ends
And the picture begins

But each goes smaller in
Faces and spangle cataract
Grace of the line of God
Behemoth who we will eat
Under lamps of her skin
On the huge table then

Some people is searching in Calcidius in his
Flat dream that happened before the gilt
Frames bought linear perspective
To make the object an object
An object is

In a familiar
Relationship.

I don't care if Blake or Dante
Ever really dreamed

But feel a sensuousness
Even for the roofs

Of the city like wax
Like pewter they shine don't they.

.

Don't they. Or the present
Is a trick of perspective.

In the city there are some walls
That rise blank in evening such that they
Are entirely undone by sky.
Below you may feel you are standing
At the lip of a void that howls
Where earth drops off sidewalk
Into this orange purple color

Nothing is.

The world is.

The world is full of this sort of thing.

.

Is that it that that
Is coming down from squared
Possibility with no break
In feeling, the medium.
The city very quiet on Saturday
There is a low echoic singing
That holds it, feeling like
Not having words for everything
All the time like Maya Deren maybe.

．

Go to brunch in Montclair New Jersey
It's my father's birthday. Everything just the same
My cousin's family won $25,000
On a game show in England.
Small talk about teaching, travel, pretend
There is an objective. Aunt Rose
Second cousin but not by blood grabs my wrist holds it
And says *that is a beautiful bracelet.*
Stroganoff or something I don't eat
The train goes past my brother's house
Over the street five times an hour.
Drank martinis and watched the Oscars
At Sam's house broke a glass when I reached for
The Doritos. He has a podcast.
Slept in Rob's bed.

ENDNOTE

In 2019, feeling lonely in the world, I wanted to write poems in the form of correspondence. At random from among those poets with whom I felt I could speak, I picked up Marie de France. She gained meaning for me, or the poems I started writing with her did, because she stands for a kind of beginning, a historicized beginning to the genre that would be called chivalric romance, one root of modern narrative. I wanted to see what would happen if I took what was strange to me about the *Lais* and wrote daily poems—a simple lyric recording my daily life in New York City in the third decade of the twenty-first century—in their key. Worrying about money, going for walks, having breakfast, reading the news. Writing under the sign of this century, in that key. Something begins appearing when certain modern narrative conventions, like a literary-historical husk, are peeled back: the revelation of a strange seed.

There are also cartographic dimensions to the *Lais*. The people in them are carried or driven here and there by forces which are beyond explanation. As this movement happens, extension happens. Worlds—complicated, angled, multiple—extend themselves around the poems according to those demands the poems unreasonably make. I am interested in this because I am interested in how worlds extend around words, in how a word might work as a device to represent worldly extension. I intended to make a book in which worlds extend into and out of the realities of words and things, to represent what isn't within what it is and *vice versa*, what's here and what could be—

[SISTE VIATOR] In the late twelfth century, the French poet and translator Marie de France writes twelve lays and a prologue. In the prologue, she claims the lays are derived from stories that circulated orally in Brittany, their purpose being, she says, to perpetuate the memory of certain adventures others had heard. She says she put them into verse in order to concentrate on "a demanding task, whereby one can ward off and rid oneself of great suffering."

[ERRANDS] In the 1430s Prince Henry of Portugal funds a series of voyages that initiate what has been called "The Age of Navigation," sending out caravels that traveled beyond the Gates of Hercules to the Azores and the coast of sub-Saharan Africa. He commissioned the Portuguese royal librarian Gomes Eannes de Azurara to write a chronicle of these voyages. The text that resulted is known as *The Discovery and Conquest of Guinea*. It depicts a familiar abomination, or one seed of it. It was modeled after classical history and medieval romance—Azurara is likely to have read Marie de France; Columbus would read his chronicle. The maps for the expeditions to Africa were made by Majorcan cartographers. Majorca was a center for mapmaking. The Majorcan style was full of symbolism, ornament and description; the maps fill in space. The world they depict is a complicated tapestry strung together on the taut fibers of the rhomb lines, radiating outwards. The compass rose first appears on a Majorcan map.

[BOUSTOPHEDON] Laura (Riding) Jackson writes the story "Reality as Port Huntlady" in Majorca in the early 1930s. Many American and European poets and writers went to Majorca in the twentieth century, following, at first, Gertrude Stein, who retreated there "to escape the war a little." Among the twentieth century English language presses and magazines that published from Majorca: Riding and Robert Graves' Seizen Press and *Epilogue*; *Caravel*; *The Mediterranean Review*; Robert Creeley's Divers Press and *Black Mountain Review*. Graves suggested Majorca might be Avalon.

—to extend a rope or tunnel of correspondence across time to another who, like me, is and isn't there in words. (Correspondence—from here to there, back and forth, between selves and speakers where self and voice undergo some kind of drag, erring in the errand.)

This is because the book I intended to make was apocalyptic, by which I mean, I meant to make a book about loving what doesn't exist, whether that nonexistent thing is a twelfth century French poet whose first name and poems are her total being in the world, her present reality, or the future of the present world, its reality.

The strange movements of language across time manifest overall an uncountable and unaccountable act of love without subject or object, because they are about millions upon millions of living and dying beings endlessly trying to talk to one another.

That's what's meant by "Marie de France." It's this stubborn talking, the undertow and marvel of it, in these apocalyptic times or any.

ACKNOWLEDGMENTS

This exists because people have taught and talked with me—some of them are:

Julie Agoos, Ammiel Alcalay, Willis Arnold, Miriam Atkin, Anselm Berrigan, Nino Bozic, Noel Capozzalo, Cricket Dean, Steven Dean, Abby Dring, Gaby Garza, August Guyot, Joshua Jones, Marika Kandelaki, Robert Kelly, Colin Kohl, Zach LaMalfa, Nate Lavey, Gracie Leavitt, Ben Lerner, James Loop, Tim Marvin, Alex Masluk, Sahar Muradi, Luned Palmer, Freya Powell, Alexis Pope, Scott Schwartz, Alan Smith, Franki Smith Palmer, Liz Roberts, Saifan Shmerer, Stacy Skolnik, Andrew Stone, Bhav Tiberwal, Michael Velasquez, Marjorie Welish, and Matvei Yankelevich.

And my family, who invented language for me.

Many thanks to the Truman Capote Foundation and Montez Press Radio for supporting this work.

Gratitude goes as well to the following magazines where some of these poems have previously appeared: *Prelude Mag*, *The Brooklyn Rail*, *Pfeil Magazine*, and many thanks to the Belladonna* Collaborative's Chaplet Series for publishing a number of these poems as a chapbook (*Apocalypses 1–12*, 2021).

CLAIRE DEVOOGD is a poet and teacher in New York City. She holds an MFA in Poetry from Brooklyn College where she was a Truman Capote Fellow. She is the author of a chaplet *Apocalypses 1–12* (Belladonna*). Other recent work can be found on Montez Press Radio, in *Prelude, The Brooklyn Rail, Pfiel,* and elsewhere. She co-edits Terrific Books, a pamphlet press.

ISBN 978-1-959708-04-9
LCCN: 2023942842

First Edition, 2023 — 800 copies

Winter Editions, Brooklyn, New York
wintereditions.net

WE books are typeset in Heldane, a renaissance-inspired serif
designed by Kris Sowersby for Klim Type Foundry, and Zirkon,
a contemporary gothic designed by Tobias Rechsteiner for Grilli
Type. The typesetting and covers are done by the editor following
a series design created by Andrew Bourne. Printed and bound in
Lithuania by BALTO print.

Winter Editions

Emily Simon, IN MANY WAYS

Garth Graeper, THE SKY BROKE MORE

Robert Desnos, NIGHT OF LOVELESS NIGHTS, tr. Lewis Warsh

Richard Hell, WHAT JUST HAPPENED

Marina Tëmkina & Michel Gérard, BOYS FIGHT
[co-published with Alder & Frankia]

Claire DeVoogd, VIA

Monica McClure, THE GONE THING

Ahmad Almallah, BORDER WISDOM

Hélio Oiticica, SECRET POETICS, tr. Rebecca Kosick
[co-published with Soberscove Press]

Heimrad Bäcker, ON DOCUMENTARY POETRY, tr. Patrick Greaney

Robert Fitterman, CREVE COEUR